# Tarts, Trams and Tuk Tuks

## A Lisbon football weekend

## by Steven Penny

First published in Great Britain in 2022

Copyright – Steven Penny 2022

Penny For Your Sports Publications

ISBN: 978-0-9541392-7-8

Pictures:
Unless stated, pictures are by the author.
Thank you to Hotel Roma and Adam Penny, plus Anton Zaitsev, Marco Verch, Vitor Oliveir, PX Fuel and Piqsels for other pictures, published under Creative Commons 2.0 licence.

*steve@stevepennymedia.co.uk*
A Penny For Your Sports production

# Contents

*Santuário de Cristo Rei's grandstand view of the Ponte 25 de Abril*  Picture: Marco Verch

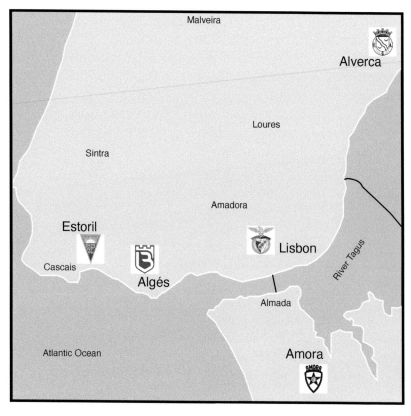

## Primeira Liga

Belenenses 0    Paços Ferreira 2
                45 Denilson (pen)
Att: 1,287       62 Ferreira

## Liga 3

Alverca 3      Torreense 1
3 Sila          64 Vilmar
42 Brandão
86 Brandão    Att: c500

## Liga 3

Amora 2       Caldas   0
11 Lourenço
14 Marcelo     Att: c300

## Primeira Liga

Benfica 3    Vitoria Guimaraes 0
23 Ramos
37 Núñez
52 Núñez    Att: 39,846

## Liga Revelação U23 play-offs

Estoril 2      Leixões 0
28 Marques
90+2 Pina    Att: c300

Adam, it's your dad. How do you fancy a weekend in Portugal to watch some football? 'What, like the other year when you dragged me halfway across Germany with a bunch of boring, middle-aged fat blokes?'

'Erm, yeah, sort of. But you were full of cold so maybe didn't enjoy it as much as me – a middle-aged fat bloke.'

'Hmm. Okay then. Yes, please.'

And so it began, one phone call and we were heading for one of Europe's top footballing destinations. A dads and lads trip to Lisbon as part of the first *Football Weekends* magazine break since Covid restrictions were eased.

Our first trip with the monthly magazine, to Germany in 2019, did indeed consist mostly of people of a certain age and body shape but did include a couple of women. This time it was all male but, much to Adam's relief, there were a couple of other lads of a similar age to him and the 'middle-aged fat blokes' he found easy to get on with.

Tickets for Sunday's match at Benfica were included in our five-day package, along with free or reduced price access to many of the city's tourist destinations for 48 hours, as well as free travel on most trains, buses and underground services in and around the city. The latter proved a real bonus, bringing the ability just to hop and off various modes of transport. There were occasional blips with some conductors refusing to recognise the tickets at first and it was not always clear which train services were and were not eligible for the offer.

Apart from the hotel and Benfica match, the rest of the itinerary was loosely formed, with the option to 'take it or leave it' for four other suggested matches. The alternative, which some other members of our group took, was to enjoy the sights and sounds of the vibrant port city of Lisbon.

Our accommodation in the handily-placed Hotel Roma in

*The Hotel Roma offered a comfortable base – and pastel de nata!* Pictures: Hotel Roma

the Alvalade district of the city was a 20-minute bus ride from the airport and all transport links were a few steps away from the front doors.

We stayed on a bed and breakfast basis and the morning meal was a veritable feast, although the full English did come in daily stages. Saturday's choice of hot dishes was scrambled egg and mushrooms, Sunday was egg and sausage, Monday we got bacon and tomatoes and Tuesday delivered sausages and hash browns. I'm sure if we'd stayed a couple of days longer we would have been offered black pudding and baked beans.

The continental offering, however, was outstanding with a real feast of fresh fruit, meat, cheeses and salads, as well as a mouth-watering selection of pastries, including the ubiquitous 'pastel de nata'. To call it a mere egg custard was doing the delicious offerings a disservice. The hotel versions, although small, were gorgeous, while the others I sampled on our journeys across this part of Portugal were equally memorable. At times I wondered if we were on a football weekend or a best bakery tour in search of these wonderful creations – not that we ever had to look that hard.

My trip had not got off to the best start. I had planned ahead and, despite living on the doorstep of Doncaster-Sheffield Airport, had to make my way to Stansted for the best flight to Humberto Delgado Aeroporto de Lisboa.

I decided to let the train take the strain as the timings were slightly quicker than by car and by booking in advance it was much cheaper.

Then along came Dudley, Eunice and Franklin to upset my plans. The trio of storms meant a check of the train schedule a few days before I was due to travel revealed that what had been a two-and-a-half hour, one-change journey, now had a four-stop strategy, much of it with the dreaded bus replacement service. Oh, and it got me to Stansted just after my flight was due to depart.

Back to the drawing board. The car it was, along with a much pricier short-notice airport parking booking and a place in my wife's bad books for commandeering our sole method of transport to abandon it in a field down south for the weekend.

While Adam relaxed on his short journey by coach across Essex, I was trundling down the A1. No problem, I'd built lots of time into my schedule and was able to linger over breakfast at Peterborough Services with plenty of time in hand.

Back on to the Great North Road and, as I'd done umpteen times before, off on to the A14 slip road via Huntingdon... ah! Except now that road doesn't go there any more does it!

I remembered too late that the A14 had been diverted on a new super smooth route. No worries I'd just stay on the old road and cut the corner. Except the 'old' road had been

*The weekend destination – British railways and the A14 allowing...*    Picture: CC2.0

returned to nature and was now a big field and the short cut was a narrow country lane with passing places. The new A14 occasionally popped by to torment me, as I crossed it and drove alongside it with no way of joining it.

Eventually, with time ticking away and visions of the 'train me' awaiting on the runway for us to wave farewell to our flight, I rejoined the old route at Cambridge Services.

Thankfully, all the bottle necks were clear and I reached my destination, far from relaxed, but with time to check-in – grateful that we were travelling light so had no need to check-in any luggage.

Panic over. The flight was smooth and when we landed it was a simple matter of collecting our travel cards and jumping on a bus to take us to the hotel.

Surely that was the drama over for this particular weekend.

Oh no – there was plenty still to come to add to a memorable and thoroughly enjoyable weekend away.

*A tantalising glimpse of the adventures that lay ahead.*     *Picture: Adam Penny.*

-11-

*The 'posh' side of the Estádio Nacional in Algés, current home of Belenenses SAD*

The opening leg of our five-match tour brought us a trip into history to the birthplace of European club competition – Portugal's national stadium, the Estádio Nacional, better known simply as Jamor.

If we thought the old Wembley was a blast from the past, the Jamor made it appear positively futuristic. It looks more like a Roman amphitheatre with its three sides of steep banked benches. The fourth side is open and offers head-spinning views towards the Atlantic coastline.

The magnificent hilltop venue may have more in common with Italy's glorious past than the ultra-modern Stadio Olimpico, but this was the very foundation of the multi-billion pound Euro Champions League.

Then known simply as the European Cup, this was where the competition's first game took place, when Sporting took on Partizan Belgrade in 1955. Their own ground was under

*The Jamor looks a lot different on one of its occasional busier days*   Picture: CC2.0

*Even in a sparsely populated state, the Jamor offers an awesome spectacle.*

*A view from the VIP seats across to the open side of the stadium* Picture: Adam Penny.

construction so the tie was played at the National Stadium. Jamor has also played host to Benfica and, until 2014 was a venue for the national team, hosting A Seleção 49 times, including 10 World Cup and European Championship qualifying fixtures, plus the quarter-final of the 1960 Euro finals. Indeed, until West Germany arrived in 1985 it had been an unconquered fortress for Portugal's World Cup qualifying campaigns.

Despite its Romanesque appearance, the stadium was actually built between 1939 and 1944, hosting its first international when Spain visited for a 1945 friendly, a year before it became home to the FA Cup final.

England won 10-0 here in a 1947 friendly – Portugal's record defeat – and 57 years later Sven-Goran Eriksson used the ground as his team's base during the 2004 Euros.

But far more memorably to British fans, particularly

*Billy McNeill lifts the UK's first European Cup and read all about it*    Pictures: CC2.0

those north of the border, it is the birthplace of lions...
the Lisbon Lions.

Celtic became the first British and northern European team to lift the European Cup in 1967 when they beat Inter Milan 2-1 in the final in front of 45,000 fans at Jamor. The ground is still a pilgrimage site for fans of the Hoops, with the iconic platform on which captain Billy McNeill lifted the famous trophy still in place.

Its current dilapidated appearance, to be fair, is not a lot different to how it has always looked and it has hosted more than 70 Taça de Portugal (Portuguese FA Cup) finals when the surrounding parkland is transformed into a giant family picnic site. There are often as many people outside the stadium's walls than in it, soaking up the atmosphere of this remarkable venue.

Perhaps the signposting is better on cup final day, but our journey for Belenenses' home match with Pacos Ferrera in the Primeira Liga was just a tad surreal.

A tram and train took us to Algés, Linda-a-Velha e Cruz Quebrada-Dafundo – thankfully much more easily described on most maps as Algés – and the Quebrada train station. From there, looking at the map on our tickets it should have been a simple walk to the entrance gate directly behind our seats.

Night had fallen so we missed the views but could hear the sea lapping up on the beach as we walked along the seafront.

That idyllic walk soon became a nightmare as we climbed over a crash barrier and had a 20-minute walk the wrong way along a dual carriageway to the ground, with cars dashing past from behind us barely inches away as we stumbled our way along the poorly surfaced hard shoulder.

Guided by the glow from the stadium floodlights high above us through the trees we eventually found the way in.

*You can't come in here... the Football Weekends party's route to Jamor is halted*

Unfortunately the gateman decided there was no entry there as it was for VIPs only, pointing behind us and saying it was a 30-minute walk back down the hill to get to the other side of the stadium – with kick-off 20 minutes away.

There was no getting past him, even though he did admit the ticket map was misleading and that "many people make this mistake". We asked politely if we could be escorted around the pitch to our seats but he was resolute – strictly no access past him.

He did suggest using a Uber and that brought a fascinating mobile phone screen race between four or five cars to get to us first – unfortunately three of them disappeared before we managed to get the first one to shuttle the group of 13 of us to the other side of the ground. When we eventually got to the correct entrance, we were stunned to discover that we had to walk around the pitch to our seats, on the same side of the ground we had just wasted all that time at. We were all of 50 yards from where we'd been refused entry and all that separated the virtually empty VIP seating from us mere mortals was a bit of string. I wonder what jobsworth is in Portuguese?

Once inside and settled in our seats – as settled as you can on a small plastic seat bolted to the concrete bench beneath it – we had chance to take in the 37,500-capacity stadium. Despite its rather primitive appearance, it was all set up for TV coverage with banks of photographers, multiple cameras, dozens of police and stewards, plus the usual moving advertising hoardings – just what you would expect for a game in the country's top league.

Unfortunately, it was all for a crowd of what looked barely 500 – although the later official figure claimed more than double that at 1,287. Although not an unusually low attendance outside the Big Three, it does come with an obvious reason for the controversial hosts, who are loaning their new home on a match-by-match basis.

Incredibly, you too could play at this historic venue, as the Jomar's website helpfully points out with a list of prices ranging from €260 for an hour of 'non-profit activity' without lights, to €900 per hour for a 'with-profits activity' under the magnificent floodlights. Belenenses, however, are believed to be handing over about €4,000 per week for the privilege.

Confusingly, the Belenenses we were watching is one of two teams with the same name. This one, although in the Primeira Liga, has no stadium of its own, has lost its club badge and has few fans.

Formed in 1919, the Belém-based club was planning to celebrate its centenary in 2018 when it was ripped in two.

*The 'other' Belenenses' Estádio do Restelo home*          *Picture: Theo K*

The fans' club divorced from the parent body, taking the ground and all assets in the settlement, but losing their league place and having to start in Lisbon regional competition. The 'official' club got just the players and their league status.

The beginnings of the split date back to 1999 when the club formed a public limited sports company (Sociedade Anónima Deportiva – SAD). That was to meet Portuguese law for clubs in the top two tiers, supposedly bringing greater financial security and transparency. In practice, however, the club sold a controlling holding to an investment fund. That inevitably led to a falling out between the two sides and, when the contract expired in 2018, the 'club' split from the SAD.

So, while, the top-level Belenenses 'SAD' rattle around in front of poor crowds at Jamor, the new fans' club – 'CF' Belenenses are attracting large followings to their 20,000-seater Estádio do Restelo home, despite playing in the fourth tier.

Ironically, the united Belenenses club had previously played at the historic Salésias ground – which was superseded as a national venue when Jamor was built.

Back to tonight's game and Jamor certainly has plenty of charm but has seen better days. Rows and rows of plastic seating bolted to the original concrete terracing, with walkways made of mosaics of small tiles and catering consisting of a man with a box of crisps, popcorn and bottles of water – for the bargain price of €2 each – walking through the crowd. There is no club shop and only basic toilet facilities.

The visitors had brought 50-or-so fans, who were vocal throughout at the far end of the single side of the ground that had been opened for the game. The home 'ultras' consisted of three women, doggedly leading a chorus of songs and chants. One mother hen-like lady in her 50s was cheerleader-

*The tale of the two Belenenses clubs is indeed a SAD story.*

in-chief with her companions being a quieter, younger one and another, bizarrely dressed as a rabbit – grey make-up, whiskers, furry costume and a mini skirt and stilettos!

A low-quality match was decided by a first-half VAR penalty from Denilson and a well-worked second-half strike courtesy of Helder Ferreira. The team sheet did need double-checking when we spotted one of the home players was called Sphephelo Sithouse – no he wasn't such a big bloke!

It was an easier walk to the station after the game, this time using a much better access road. Just to add to the night's entertainment, we were engulfed by a group of 30 lederhosen-clad hikers, complete with huge rucksacks, who emerged from a bush and, just as swiftly disappeared into the night down an alley. Swiss walkers and a bunny girl – quite a night!

*Trams of all shapes and sizes ply their trade on the streets of Lisbon*

J ust the one afternoon game today brought the chance for sightseeing and Lisbon delivered plenty of surprises – it is very hilly, has some amazing city squares and statues, with plenty of stunning buildings and lovely estuary-side views, as well as a couple of incredible bridges. Trams of all shapes, sizes and colours are everywhere – like Blackpool on speed!

As for the football, we were going to see a Liga 3 encounter, Alverca versus Torreense and a pre-match pint or two delivered an unexpected bonus when the barman asked if we'd got anything planned for 3pm. He promptly handed over free tickets for the game we were going to. 1-0!

A short walk to the ground and just in time for a quick Super Bock at only €2 a pint and an amazing homemade burger and chips. 2-0!

*A restricted view of the action – thankfully the home end was not a long walk*

After another 'you can't come in here' crisis, we were directed to the home end – thankfully just a two-minute walk after last night's débâcle – alongside the sad sight of the club's derelict former ground. Who should we spot zealously protecting the bar in the stadium? None other than last night's 'border guard' – none shall pass. Boo! 2-1

However, he couldn't sour the atmosphere this time and we witnessed a cracking promotion clash between Alverca and Torreense, which went 3-1 in favour of the hosts. Yes, 3-1!

It looked a similar-sized crowd to the previous night but this time the fans were in one small stand, complete with roof, creating a buoyant atmosphere with two sets of home 'ultras' competing with each other from either end – a truly stereo experience.

Despite the sun and we Brits being suitably attired in shorts and T-shirts, the locals were still in standard winter garb, with lots of jumpers and coats in evidence. They must have been sweltering, it was a glorious day.

I thought I might blend in with a home shirt but merely identified myself as a tourist! The Barcelona-esque shirt was

*Tuck in – not a tart this time!*　　　　*Are you Barcelona in disguise?*

*All wrapped up to cope with the Portuguese weather*

bought from the bar. All I asked was if they had a club shop and two minutes later the barman turned up with a selection of goodies to choose from. How could I refuse?

On the pitch, Onyekachi Silas opened the scoring with a header after Brazilian Klismahn's shot had crashed off the cross bar three minutes in, with a double from Evandro Brandão completing matters either side of Vilmar's 64th-minute reply.

Today's highlight on the team sheet? The home left back was called David Dinamite... boom! Meanwhile, the home coaches went by the barely believable names of Argel Fucks and Fernando Orge.

Alverca spent four seasons in the Primeira Liga from 1998 to 2002 and again in 2003/4 but it is in their current guise in Liga 3 that they made a name for themselves, becoming only the second team from the third tier in history, and the first since Tirsense in 1948, to knock Sporting out of the Portuguese Cup, stunning the giants 2-0 in 2019.

Sadly, Alex Apolinário, who scored the opening goal in that

match died in January 2021, four days after suffering a heart attack during Alverca's game with Almeirim. The Brazilian was just 24.

From Alverca it was a return to the hotel via a stop in L'Orient to have a look at Europe's second-longest bridge – the 10-mile long Vasco da Gama Bridge, an incredible sight appearing like a string of beads hanging across the Tagus estuary. The viewing area was in a park, complete with a display of flags from every country in the world, various works of art, including a 60-foot cat made of waste plastic, a cable car, oh, and a group of Hari Krishna worshippers on the foreshore just for today's dash of surrealism.

Yes, it's been another cracking day on our Portuguese Football Weekend.

Big one tomorrow – an 11am kick-off at Amora for my 500th different football ground in almost half a century of watching the sport live, before heading back across the water for the main event – Benfica and a 6pm kick-off.

*The sorry sight of Alverca's old ground, which you pass on the way to the new one*

*Flying the flag. Home fans under cover and the wide open spaces opposite*

*1-0 – Fans celebrate Amora's opening goal against Caldas*

*2-0 – no time to sit down before the hosts double their advantage*

Sunday and a day of rest – yeah right! Another event-packed day on our Lisbon Football Weekend and, it being a holy day, a bit of religion too.

Having worked out which train to catch to go south of the River Tagus for Amora's Liga 3 clash with Caldas – made just a bit difficult with the complete lack of signs or timetables at the station – we were a little concerned when a 'priest' appeared in the carriage.

He was in full-on Vatican gear and rattled off a lengthy 'sermon'. No idea what it was about and it raised not even a glance from the other passengers. Just as quickly as he appeared, he was gone. Was it a mirage?

The town of Amora is in the Setúbal district and the club now plays in a converted athletic stadium – the Complexo Municipal de Atletismo Carla Sacramen. Amora reached the heights of the Primeira League for three seasons in the early 1980s after earning promotion as Segunda Divisão champions

*United nations – Flags of the world, erm... a giant cat and the impressive 10-mile long*

*ama Bridge with a cable car running alongside the neighbouring park*

Tarts, Trams and Tuk Tuks

*Parking the bus – no trams, tuk tuks or even trains for today's two teams*

under Félix Mourinho – José's father. Despite being formed in 1921, those three seasons were their only ones at the highest level and they have since shuttled mainly between levels three and four.

The ground is visible as you enter the town and meant a half-hour walk back through what looks like an industrial area in the making.

This morning's appetiser, despite it seeing me hit my landmark ground, was really to build up a thirst for the day's main event at Benfica – quite literally it turned out.

All drinks containers were confiscated at the entrance gate and, to our dismay, despite the blazing heat of the day, there were no drinks or refreshments of any kind available inside the ground. British health & safety would have had a field day, even more so when they spotted the precarious spiral staircase for the main exit.

All the fans were housed in an open stand with the only shade being a series of gazebo structures covering the VIPs and press sections – where bottles of water were being casually handed out (oh, how I wish I'd brought my press pass with me!). A small group of home Ultras gathered at the top

*Soaking up the sun in Amora – just don't expect to find any water*

# Tarts, Trams and Tuk Tuks

*Two Lisbon treasures: Santuário de Cristo Rei overlooking the Ponte 25 de Abril*

*Stand still long enough and you too could get covered in graffiti*     Pictures: CC2.0

of the seats, with small clutches of vocal and chanting fans scattered in and among the largely family crowd of about 300.

Gildo Lourenço and Paulo Marcelo grabbed two early goals for the home side to raise hopes of a goal feast. However, their work done, they then sat back and absorbed the Caldas pressure. But, apparently, wait for it... that's Amora. Sorry!

The game burst back into life in the last few minutes with both teams blazing over open goals.

Today's jungle drum moment on the team sheets? That goes to Caldas' No.32 João Tarzan.

The walk back to the station brought the relief of grabbing a welcome bottle of water before the chance to admire the amazing views of Lisbon from the Ponte 25 de Abril (25th April Bridge) and also some incredible graffiti – every surface in the city seems covered in it – mainly walls but occasionally vans that had stayed too long in one place!

A quick change and it was back out for the day's main course – Benfica here we come.

*It ain't half hot – fans keep out the sun any way they can*

*Duck! Eagle on the loose. The Benfica mascot's lap of honour ahead of kick-off*

*Bird's eye view – the Benfica eagle returns to the ground*     Picture: Anton Zaitsev

We knew which bus we needed to catch but the direction was a guess – thankfully the sight of floodlights soon eased any concerns we were heading the wrong way. The green exterior of the Sporting stadium, however, was not what we were aiming for! A quick check of the map and, phew, yes, Benfica's fierce neighbours were on the route to Da Luz.

Eventually the correct ground hove into view – a glorious red edifice. The amazing Estádio da Luz – once boasting the largest capacity in Europe at 120,000. The stadium was rebuilt in 2003, offering an all-seated 65,000 capacity and a stunning spectacle. As well as Benfica's legendary European nights, it has also hosted the Portuguese national team 23 times and five Euro 2004 matches, including the final. The highest home attendance record was set in 2017 – 64,519 spectators witnessing Benfica's 5–0 win over Vitória de Guimarães in the season's last match. Coincidentally today's opponents.

One of the nation's big three, Benfica have never been relegated from the top level, alongside Sporting and Porto. Sixth place in 2001 is the lowest they've ever finished and third place last season was the first time outside the top two since a similar finish in 2009. Whisper it quietly but Porto have finished in the top three every season since 1976!

The Eagles are the most supported Portuguese club and also the European club with the highest percentage of supporters in their own country – with more than 250,000 members and about 14 million supporters worldwide. Benfica are the most

*Roll up! Roll up! The pre-match atmosphere (and selling) builds*

decorated club in Portugal with 84 trophies to their name, including a record 37 Primeira titles. They were also European Cup winners in 1961 and '62, finishing as runners-up in 1963, '65, '68, '88 and '90.

Although they are regarded as the working class club of Portugal, the contrast between their facilities and those at most of the 15 outside the big three is incredible – to compare it to the situation in England, think Premier League versus Northern Premier League. While the Big Three were averaging more than 43,000 fans per game, pre-Covid, Tondela's aggregate after 13 matches this season is a mere 12,646, with a season's low of just 439 for the visit of Famalicão.

A swift glance at our tickets and ID by the security team got us into the ground, only to realise the Fan Zone was back outside. Out we went to witness a queue of about 300 people, I assumed for tickets. However, they were waiting to cheer the home team bus when it arrived on the roadway below into the bowels of the stadium – perhaps also just checking they had turned up!

*Inspiring artwork on the way to the Estádio da Luz*

Large groups gathered around various stages with fans taking their turn to sing a multitude of club songs, enthusiastically backed by a screeching pair of wannabe DJs. Dozens of food and drink kiosks were enjoying a busy time, with long queues also into the club superstore.

A junior match on the adjacent artificial turf pitch gave fans an early taste of live action. There was a real family day out vibe to proceedings and that continued inside the ground.

Arsenal's Emirates Stadium is based on Benfica's stadium and the similarities were striking. One huge difference, however, is that the London club do not have their own pet eagle soaring above the crowd in spectacular style as part of the pre-match entertainment. A cartoon version acts as the club mascot and he was kept busy posing for pre-match pictures with young fans.

A variety of club hymns and anthems then followed with

*Benfica fans celebrate a goal against Vitória de Guimarães*

*A wall of red scarves, punctuated by blue and yellow Ukraine flags at Da Luz*

a mass scarf waving display reducing the temperature significantly – a brilliant air conditioning system on what was another warm evening!

For most fans, Benfica is a religion and they follow their club with complete devotion. With the vast majority of the near 40,000 fans supporting the home team, visitors Vitória de Guimarães could only muster a handful – hidden away behind a giant net in the rafters of the 65,000-capacity Estádio Lisboa e Benfica da Luz, to give it its full name.

Benfica were the last Portuguese club to allow foreigners to play for them – not until 1979 – but the current first-team squad of 27 players has just eight Portuguese. Six are from Brazil with the rest coming from Serbia, Spain, Belgium, Uruguay, France, Switzerland, Austria, Germany, Argentina, Morocco, Greece and Ukraine, of whom more later.

Scarves were held aloft, before kick-off, for a deafening rendition of the club anthem, creating a cauldron of noise.

It was the red-shirted hosts who made the early running but the two best chances fell to Vitoria, who were denied by superb blocks from goalkeeper Odysseas Vlachodimos. They were made to pay for those misses when Gonçalo Ramos crashed home the opening goal to set the stadium alight.

Darwin Núñez added a double to complete a 3-0 win but the biggest and most emotional cheer of the night was reserved for the arrival of substitute Roman Yaremchuk, with the Ukrainian reduced to tears by his greeting. Russia had recently invaded his country and in many signs of unity, the yellow and blue flag was prominent around the stadium.

A surprisingly smooth departure from the stadium allowed an earlier than expected trip to the Magic Pool bar for a catch-up chat with the rest of our party.

A bonus came with the sight of 'IPA' proudly emblazoned on one of the pumps – yes, Portuguese lager

*A sea of red as Benfica fans pay tribute to their heroes*

*No need to be bitter – it's an away win!*

makers Super Bok do a bitter!

So far our fleeting meetings with the rest of the Football Weekends magazine tour party had been limited to just the chance to discuss favourite teams – hence we only knew each other by our clubs: Scarborough, Tottenham, Dartford, Torquay, South Shields, Newcastle and Tranmere, as well as the 'American guy', the Italian and the Irish Daddy, among them.

So a delightful few hours were spent discovering more about Mark 'Tranmere' and his zealous groundhopping adventures, the relationship between geographically puzzling travelling companions Torquay and Dartford – they are father and son Ian and Ellis – and an enthralling chat with our trans-Atlantic guest Jim. He is chaplain at a hospital and had a great and humbling tale to tell of his work with the multi-faith team at the world famous London establishment.

Yes, despite Adam's concerns that he would be on a trip with fat, old, football bores, it was actually quite an eclectic and interesting gathering.

Tarts, Trams and Tuk Tuks

*Just for funicular? Specially built trams ascend Lisbon's steep streets*   Picture: CC2.0

Our last day gave a chance to do something different. An electric trike 'tuk tuk' tour of the old city of Lisbon took us through the narrow, busy, streets, where sunshine struggles to find its way in before immediately turning a corner into the wide open hilltop vistas for spectacular views across this glorious city.

Panoramas took in São Jorge Castle, the Ponte 25 de Abril and the oft derided Santuário de Cristo Rei statue on the far bank of the River Tagus. As our guide told us: "We are proud Portuguese and we do not want cheap imitations of another country's glories." In this case Rio's Christ the Redeemer monument.

Different parts of the city have contrasting allegiances – Benfica or Sporting. I was pleased I'd decided to stay neutral today although had second thoughts about how wise my choice was of a Lanzarote top. It was pointed out how Portugal had always been friends with England, thanks to our

*Tuk tuk in... modern trikes compete with trams for tourist trade*     Picture: CC2.0

*Cathedral ruins (*Picture: CC2.0*), top, and a view across the city, above*

*Lisbon's impressive Praça do Comércio, one of Portugal's largest plazas*

help in wars against France ...and Spain. Oops!

The tour took in the medieval city before venturing into the 'new' part of city, built after the horrors of 1755. We saw the derelict cathedral left after an earthquake killed many in the congregation. Survivors fled towards the river, only to be drowned by a tsunami. In total about 60,000 city residents lost their lives that November day.

We also drove past the national parliament buildings, complete with a tent city of protesters outside, before heading to a restaurant for a traditional Portuguese 'petiscos' meal. A tapas-like selection of fish dishes, cheeses, vegetables, meats and olives, etc, was fed to us in procession, washed down by local wine before an ice cream and chocolate finale.

This was the final event for many of our party so a farewell quiz was organised. Adam and I finished fourth (yes, there were only four teams) but we claimed victory by dint of having one fewer member than the other teams so won on

*Lisbon roof lines, top, and the Portuguese parliament building, with tent city*

*A ferry near miss... a rush to catch the train almost saw the travellers take to sea*

'points average' – I'm not sure the other teams or question master agreed, however. I also disputed one question as to which was the second biggest team in Porto – surely it should be Porto reserves rather than Boavista? (Copyright: Bill Shankly when referring to Liverpool Reserves and Everton I believe?)

Then followed a rush to the railway station for the remaining five members of our party for the chance to get in some 'beach' time – 'praia' in the native tongue – or Estoril Praia to give the club we were going to watch their full name.

Unfortunately our 'travel anywhere' tickets would not open the barrier so we had to queue at the ticket office... only to find it was for the ferry across the river. Once located on the correct mode of transport, it was another journey along the beachside line, serenaded by a busking rap artist, and a half-hour walk up the pleasant but steep streets of Estoril, keeping our fingers crossed that there was actually a game on and that we'd be allowed entry – there was doubts as to exactly where the u23 championship play-off against Leixões would take place and if spectators would be allowed.

Formed in 1939, it is one of many signs that Portugal was

neutral for much of the Second World War, along with Jamor's 1939-1944 construction dates.

Thankfully, our final game was indeed to be played at the Primeira Liga club's 8,000-capacity Estádio António Coimbra da Mota and not only were fans welcome, admission was free.

Estoril chose yellow and blue as their formation colours to represent the local beaches and sea. Those colours remain prominent around the ground and adjacent club shop.

The club competed in the Europa League in 2012/13 and '13/14, also achieving a fourth-place finish in the Primeira Liga in that second season. However, this season is their first back in the top division after a three-year stint one level lower.

Their best-known manager was probably Durham-born England international Jimmy Hagan. He also managed Benfica, Sporting, Vitoria de Setúbal, Belenenses and Boavista and was a big friend of Eusebio.

The odd kick-off time, 5pm on a work day meant we were not

*A late rush saw about 300 people turn up to watch Estoril u23s*

*Impressive 'executive boxes' at Estádio António Coimbra da Mota*

expecting a huge crowd and, sure enough, 20 minutes before kick-off the Football Weekends tour quintet formed half the crowd. However, surprisingly and seemingly from nowhere, by the start the attendance was a healthy 300-or-so.

Despite a bank of 'executive boxes' opposite, actually a block of flats towering over the ground, there seemed to be no additional spectators to add to the tally. Just the one covered stand was open, with a large bank of seating behind one goal and a half-dozen tiers of seating opposite us, awaiting the visit of far bigger opponents.

It looked as if our goals record would be ended. Having seen a 3-0 win, a 3-1 and two 2-0s, this one had 0-0 written all over it. A very scrappy game was played at practice match pace with neither team able to string more than two passes together.

Then, out of the blue 28 minutes in, fans' chants of 'attacka, attacka' and 'shoota, shoota' were rewarded when João

*Estoril Praia supporters have made sure their territory is well marked*

Marques crashed the ball into the net for the hosts.

That was the end of the action in a low-quality match until the second minute of stoppage time when the hosts doubled their advantage through Rúben Pina, just as I was leaving to buy an Estoril sweatshirt to cover my Lanzarote top for the journey back to the hotel.

Again the crowd seemed to vanish into the night and it was hard to imagine that this quiet seaside town was fielding a team in the Primeira Liga. How different it must look when the travelling hordes from Portugal's big three visit.

And so, after a brief discussion about the unusual Leixões badge – it's a combination of a football, cricket bat and tennis racquet, showing the early English influence on the Portuguese game – it was back to the hotel for the final time. Packing done it was off to the airport early Tuesday morning for the flight home.

Break over it was time to get home – the easy part surely? After a quick dash to the nearest bakery to pick up some pastel de nata to offer some compensation to my wife for the loss of her car for the weekend – well that was the plan but time spent waiting in the airport meant I might have had a little nibble... or two. Crumbs!

Lisbon airport has two terminals but only one bus stop and poor signposting. We dashed in only to have our boarding cards refused and ushered out to a waiting bus. Herded on board and carted off to who knows where, panic started to set in among some of the other travellers. However, we were actually on the way to the terminal we needed to be at – oblivious to the fact it even existed before then. From the calm and quiet one we had left, we were now thrust into a virtual cattle market.

Long queues led to temperatures fraying and we learned lots of new swear words in a variety of languages as several people tried to ignore the snakes of passengers awaiting security and simply walked through the middle.

It was all very entertaining, knowing we had plenty of time to enjoy the free entertainment being laid on for us and with a few morsels of pastel de nata to finish off ahead of our flight.

I can't do anything about being middle-aged but I wonder if Adam might have spotted why I am a little overweight? Too much time spent on trams and tuk tuks perhaps?

The author travelled with a Football Weekends break to Lisbon at the end of February 2022. The cost for the four-night break, which included accommodation at the 3* Hotel Roma on a bed and breakfast basis was £379 (based on two people sharing a twin room) – this also included a Lisboa Card, offering unlimited free travel by bus, metro, tram, 'elevadores' and some trains for 48 hours, as well as free or discounted admission to museums, attractions and tours. The card normally retails at €35 (€44 for a 72-hour card). A separate Lisbon travel card was included as part of the break for the remaining time. Other benefits of the break included a welcome drink, a city tuk tuk tour and lunch on the final day.

Match tickets for Benfica versus Vitoria Guimaraes were part of the package. There was an extra charge for entry to matches at Beleneses (€20), Alverca (two for €10 – but on this occasion, free) and Amora (€5) but admission to Estoril u23s was free.

Ryanair tickets from Stansted to Humberto Delgado Aeroporto de Lisboa were £46.80 return, plus £56.15 for car parking in the long-stay facility (booked at short notice).

**Useful websites:**

Visit Lisbon – *www.visitlisboa.com/en*

Lisboa Card – *www.lisboacard.org*

Transport: Metro – *www.metrolisboa.pt/en*

Buses – *www.carris.pt/en*

Hotel Roma – *www.hotelroma.pt/en*

Others – *www.lisbonguru.com* – *www.lisbon.net*

Football Weekends magazine – www.*footballweekends.co.uk*

Football clubs:

Benfica – *www.slbenfica.pt/en-us*

Sporting – *www.sporting.pt/en*

Benfica and Sporting play at home on alternative weekends and have regular midweek matches so you should always be able to book a weekend stay and see one or other in action – however, check their website early for ticket availability.

There are many clubs within easy travel time in and around Lisbon and four of these play at the top level, the Primeira Liga – Benfica, Sporting, Belenenses SAD and Estoril.

In Liga 2, there are five clubs within a 25-mile radius – Casa Pia, Estrela da Amadora, Mafra and Vilafranquense, as well as Benfica B.

Liga 3 gives you another five options –Alverca, Amora, Cova da Piedade, Oriental Dragon and Sporting B.

Below that, the Campeonato de Portugal offers another seven options, including Pinhalnovense at the other end of the magnificent 10-mile long Vasco da Gama Bridge. The others are: Barreirense, CF Belenenses, Loures, Pêro Pinheiro, Sacavenense and Sintrense.

Below that are two tiers of the Lisbon District FA, not to mention the various women's and youth clubs around the city, plus a thriving u23 competition.

Fixtures and table for most of these competitions are available on the excellent Soccerway website – *uk.soccerway. com/national/portugal*

(* All information correct April 2022)

Tarts, Trams and Tuk Tuks

Also by this author

# Towering Tales & a Ripping Yarn
## Yorkshire football's grassroots legends

Football writer Steven Penny takes you on a journey across the football fields of Yorkshire during the 2020/21 season, discovering some incredible links to the game's greats.

Liverpool, Manchester United and Arsenal are among 90 professional clubs from the UK who have links to the lower-level Yorkshire clubs featured in this book. Add a sprinkle of overseas clubs and international teams, including England's 1966 World Cup winners, and the grassroots scene in the Broad Acres has given much to the global game.

Discover the story of the world's first black professional footballer, the pop star who arranged his gigs to carry on playing Sunday football and the White Rose apprenticeship served by managerial legends Bill Shankly, Joe Harvey and Herbert Chapman. Read about the schoolboy footballers who conquered the world and the fictional team that went down a storm in a TV classic.

Penny digs up dozens of tremendous tales of life on the White Rose county's lesser-known football fields.

---

# Soap Stars & Burst Bubbles
## A season of Yorkshire football

Football writer Steven Penny takes you on a journey across the football fields of Yorkshire during the 2002/03 season.

From the multi-national squad of Premiership club Middlesbrough to the six-year-old boys of Wheldrake Junior FC playing their first game.

The book concentrates on the non-League clubs of the county, from Barnoldswick – playing in Lancashire competitions – to Easington – tucked away on Spurn Point. And from Northern League sides Marske United and Northallerton Town to the world's oldest club, Sheffield FC, now based in Derbyshire.

Penny reports on more than 40 matches, including Harrogate Railway's remarkable FA Cup run and Doncaster Rovers' return to the Football League. As well as reports and match details from every game, included are club histories, interviews with fans and club officials as well as stories from Penny's trips around the county and his long non-League football pedigree.

*Both books are available from Amazon*
*as paperback or ebooks*

-57-